OXFORD SPELLING

Dr Tessa Daffern

STUDENT BOOK

F

Name: _____

Class: _____

OXFORD
UNIVERSITY PRESS
AUSTRALIA & NEW ZEALAND

OXFORD
UNIVERSITY PRESS

Oxford University Press is a department of the University of Oxford.
It furthers the University's objective of excellence in research,
scholarship, and education by publishing worldwide. Oxford is a registered
trademark of Oxford University Press in the UK and in certain other
countries.

Published in Australia by
Oxford University Press
Level 8, 737 Bourke Street, Docklands, Victoria 3008, Australia.

© Oxford University Press 2021

ISBN 9780190326081

Reproduction and communication for educational purposes
The Australian *Copyright Act 1968* (the Act) allows educational institutions that
are covered by remuneration arrangements with Copyright Agency to reproduce
and communicate certain material for educational purposes. For more information,
see copyright.com.au.

Edited by Lucy Ridsdale
Cover illustration by Lisa Hunt
Illustrated by Villie Karabatzia and Tom Heard
Typeset by Integra Software Services Pvt. Ltd., Pondicherry, India
Proofread by Anita Mullick
Printed in China by Leo Paper Products Ltd

Acknowledgements
Extract, *Never Mail an Elephant*, by Mike Thaler, Hinkler Books, 1994 p. 102; Extract, *Alexander's Outing* by Pamela
Allen. Text copyright © Pamela Allen. First published by Puffin 1994, reprinted by permission of Penguin Random
House Australia Pty Ltd, p. 77; Extract, *Mr McGee Goes to Sea*, by Pamela Allen. Text copyright © Pamela Allen.
First published by Picture Puffin 1993, reprinted by permission of Penguin Random House Australia Pty Ltd,
p. 105; Extract, *Mr McGee and the Big Bag of Bread* by Pamela Allen. First published by Penguin Random House
Australia Pty Ltd, 2004; Extract, *A Squash and a Squeeze* by Julia Donaldson, MacMillan Children's Books, 2004;
Extract, *Wombat Stew* by Marcia Vaughan, Scholastic Books, 1984, p. 101; *A Job for Jump-bot* by Cameron Macintosh,
Oxford University Press, Reading for Comprehension 2019; *Happy Diwali* by Janine Scott, Oxford University
Press, Reading for Comprehension 2019; *My Family Helps Me* by Gordon Coutts, Oxford University Press, Reading
for Comprehension, 2019; *The Dentist Can Help You* by George Ivanoff, Oxford University Press, Reading for
Comprehension 2019.

The 'Bringing it together' activities provided online are adapted with permission from Daffern, T. (2018).
The components of spelling: Instruction and assessment for the linguistic inquirer. Literacy Education Solutions Pty Limited.

Every effort has been made to trace the original source of copyright material contained in this book.
The publisher will be pleased to hear from copyright holders to rectify any errors or omissions.

WELCOME TO OXFORD SPELLING

Welcome to *Oxford Spelling Student Book F*! This book contains 28 units that you will use across the year, and that will help you gain new spelling knowledge and skills.

You will notice that each unit is divided into three sections:

- **Phonology (green section)**
- **Orthography (blue section)**
- **Morphology (purple section).**

This has been done to guide you in the types of thinking you might use to answer the questions in each section.

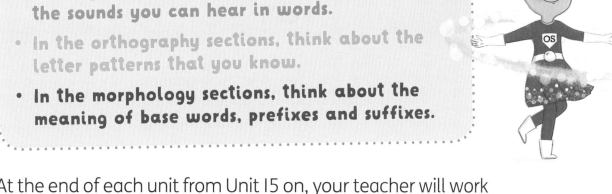

Tip

- In the phonology sections, think about the sounds you can hear in words.
- In the orthography sections, think about the letter patterns that you know.
- In the morphology sections, think about the meaning of base words, prefixes and suffixes.

At the end of each unit from Unit 15 on, your teacher will work with you on a 'Bringing it together' activity. This is a chance to bring together all the things you are learning about spelling and apply them to new words!

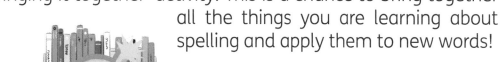

Your teacher, along with the *Oxford Spelling* superheroes, will be giving you lots of helpful information as you work through this book. Look out for the tips in each unit for handy hints on how to answer questions.

Enjoy *Oxford Spelling,* and meet the two superheroes who will help you become super spellers - Bubbly Bo and Colourful Cal!

UNIT 1

Tip

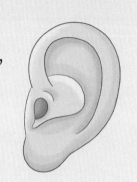

A phoneme is the smallest speech sound that you can hear in a word.

The word 'bat' has three phonemes: **/b/**, **/a/** and **/t/**.
When you see letters with lines on either side, such as **/b/**, it describes the speech sound.

A vowel is a sound made by opening your mouth and not blocking with your teeth or tongue.

The vowel phoneme in the word 'bat' is **/a/**.

1 Say the word you can see in the picture. Can you hear the phoneme **/s/**? Colour the pictures with the phoneme **/s/**. Write the letter **s** below those pictures.

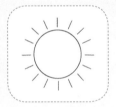     

_____ _____ _____ _____ _____ _____

2 Say the word you can see in the picture. Can you hear the phoneme **/a/**? Colour the pictures with the phoneme **/a/**. Write the letter **a** below those pictures.

_____ _____ _____ _____ _____ _____

OXFORD UNIVERSITY PRESS

3 Say the word you can see in the picture. Can you hear the phoneme **/t/**? Colour the pictures with the phoneme **/t/**. Write the letter **t** below those pictures.

_____ _____ _____ _____ _____ _____

4 Say the word you can see in the picture. Can you hear the phoneme **/p/**? Colour the pictures with the phoneme **/p/**. Write the letter **p** below those pictures.

_____ _____ _____ _____ _____ _____

5 Say each word. What is the first phoneme?
Draw a line to match each word with its first phoneme.

| at | tap | pat | sat |

/s/   /a/   /p/   /t/

6 Use the letter **s** or **p** to make words that end with **at**.

_____at   _____at

1 My first name is:

_____

2 Point to each letter of the alphabet. Say the name of each letter. Colour the letters of the alphabet that are in your first name.

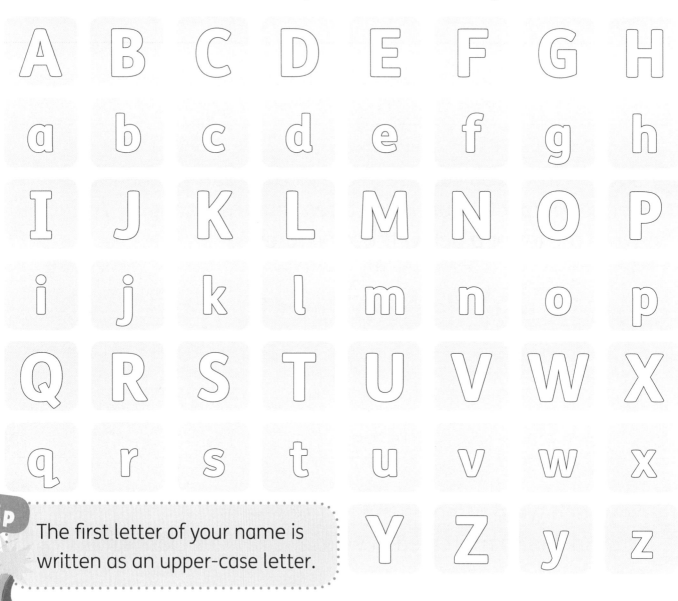

A B C D E F G H
a b c d e f g h
I J K L M N O P
i j k l m n o p
Q R S T U V W X
q r s t u v w x
Y Z y z

Tip The first letter of your name is written as an upper-case letter.

3 Write the missing letter **s** in each word. Say each word. Can you hear the phoneme **/s/**?

_____ank   _____ea   be_____ide   _____it

4 Write the missing letter **a** in each word. Say each word. Can you hear the phoneme **/a/**?

s_____t   _____t   b_____t   th_____t

5 Write the missing letter **t** in each word. Say each word. Can you hear the phoneme **/t/**?

boa_____   i_____   tha_____   ge_____

6 Write the missing letter **p** in each word. Say each word. Can you hear the phoneme **/p/**?

_____lace   _____in   shee_____   _____art

A plural is a word for two or more things.
The word 'hats' is the plural of 'hat'.

Tip

1 Write the missing word. Add the letter **s** to show there is more than one thing.

Here is one tap.

Here are two _____.

1 Say the word you can see in the picture. Can you hear the phoneme **/i/**? Colour the pictures with the phoneme **/i/**. Write the letter **i** below those pictures.

    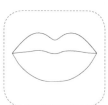 

_____   _____   _____   _____   _____   _____

2 Say the word you can see in the picture. Can you hear the phoneme **/n/**? Colour the pictures with the phoneme **/n/**. Write the letter **n** below those pictures.

_____   _____   _____   _____   _____   _____

3 Draw a line to match each picture and word:

pin

pan

OXFORD UNIVERSITY PRESS

4 Say each word. Circle the words that start with the phoneme **/n/**. Draw a line under the words that end with the phoneme **/n/**.

tin   nap   pan   nip

5 Write the letter **t**, **p** or **n** on each line to make a word that ends with the letters **an**.

_____an   _____an

6 Circle the letters that you can use to make a word that ends with the letters **in**.

t   p   n

Write a letter on each line to make a word that ends with **in**.

_____in   _____in

7 Say each word. How many phonemes can you hear? Write the word in the correct box.

sit   it   spin   pant   at   nap

Two phonemes	Three phonemes	Four phonemes

OXFORD UNIVERSITY PRESS

1 Write each word twice.

look ➤ say ➤ cover ➤ write ➤ check

a

at

it

in

is

as

an

I

1 Write the missing word. Remember to add the letter **s** to show there is more than one thing.

a Here is one pan. Here are two _____.

b Here is one pin. Here are two _____.

c Here is one ant. Here are two _____.

UNIT 3

1 Say the word you can see in the picture. Can you hear the phoneme **/m/**? Colour the pictures with the phoneme **/m/**. Write the letter **m** below those pictures.

_____   _____   _____   _____   _____

2 Say the word you can see in the picture. Can you hear the phoneme **/d/**? Colour the pictures with the phoneme **/d/**. Write the letter **d** below those pictures.

_____   _____   _____   _____   _____

3 Say each word. Circle the words that start with the phoneme **/m/**. Draw a line under the words that start with the phoneme **/d/**.

| map | dam | mist | dip | did | mad |

4 Read the letters below. Write a letter on each line to make words that end with the letters *it*.

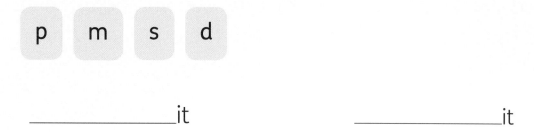

p m s d

_____it   _____it

5 Read the letters. Write a letter on each line to make words that end with the letters *ip*.

s t m d

_____ip   _____ip

6 Say each word. How many phonemes can you hear? Circle the words with three phonemes. Draw a line under the words with four phonemes.

sat   spit   tip   span   and   pans

dip   man   sip   spin   stab

OXFORD UNIVERSITY PRESS

1 Write each word twice.

look → say → cover → write → check

and		
am		
dad		
did		
is		
as		
I		

Tip

Some words sound the same but look different and have a different meaning. These words are called homophones.

The words 'to', 'too' and 'two' are homophones.

1 Read this sentence. Circle the homophones.

I spy with my little eye.

2 Write the missing word. Remember to add the letter **s** to show there is more than one thing.

a One mat   Two_____

b One eye   Two_____

1 Say the word you can see in the picture. Can you hear the phoneme **/g/**? Colour the pictures with the phoneme /g/. Write the letter **g** below those pictures.

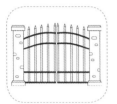    

——————— ——————— ——————— ——————— ———————

Tip

Vowels can have different sounds. Short vowels are:

/a/ as in <u>a</u>nt  **/e/** as in <u>e</u>gg

/i/ as in <u>i</u>gloo 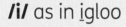 **/o/** as in <u>o</u>ctopus

/u/ as in <u>u</u>mbrella

2 Say the word you can see in the picture. Can you hear the **short /o/** vowel phoneme? Colour the pictures with the **short /o/** phoneme. Write the letter **o** below those pictures.

——————— ——————— ——————— ——————— ———————

3 Say each word:

got dig gap dog

OXFORD UNIVERSITY PRESS

Now, write the word in the correct box.

Starts with /g/	Ends with /g/

> **Tip**
>
> A medial phoneme is a sound in the middle of a word.
> The word 'cat' has a medial /a/ phoneme.

4 Say each word. Draw a line under the words that have the phoneme **/o/** in the middle. Circle the words that have the phoneme **/a/** in the middle.

pot   tag   got   sat   dog   sag

5 Read the letters. Write one letter in each box to make three new words.

p   m   s   d   g

Onset	Rime
	ot
	op
	og

6 Write the missing letters in each sentence.

I see a d ___ ___.

I see a fr ___ ___.

The rabbits h___ ___.

They cannot st___ ___.

1 Write each word twice.

⭐ OXFORD WORDLIST   look ⟶ say ⟶ cover ⟶ write ⟶ check

on		
to		
not		
go		
got		
dog		

Orthography

1 Write the homophone 'to' in these sentences. They are based on a book called *A Job for Jump-bot* by Cameron Macintosh.

a I like _____ help.

b I like _____ clean.   c I like _____ cook.

2 Write the homophone 'two' in these sentences.

a Jump-bot has _____ hands.

b Jump-bot has _____ eyes.

c Jump-bot has _____ arms.

3 Write the missing words. Remember to add the letter **s** to show there is more than one thing.

a I have one dog.   I have two _____.

b I have one pot.   I have two _____.

1 Say the word you can see in the picture. Can you hear the phoneme **/k/**? Colour the pictures with the phoneme **/k/**. Write the letter **k** below those pictures.

_____ _____ _____ _____ _____

Tip

The **/k/** phoneme can be written in different ways.
It can be written with the letters **k**, **c** or **ck**.

2 Say each word. Circle the letter or letters that stand for the phoneme **/k/**.

| cat | kite | sack | stick |

3 Write the word in the correct box.

Starts with **/k/** phoneme	Ends with **/k/** phoneme

OXFORD UNIVERSITY PRESS

4 Say each word. Write the letter **s** on each line below to make the words.

| sick | sock | sack |

_____ick   _____ock   _____ack

Tip

One phoneme can sometimes be written using two letters. This is called a digraph.

In the word 'duck', the letters **ck** are a digraph.

1 Say each word. Which letter or letters stand for the phoneme **/k/**? Circle them in these words. Write one correct word in each box below.

| can | kite | sock | pack | like | cap | kit | cat | sick |

A word with **c**	A word with **k**	A word with **ck**

The digraph **ck** is never used at the start of a word.

2 Write each word twice.

look ····▶ say ····▶ cover ····▶ write ····▶ check

can		
cat		
said		
like		
sick		

1 Fill in the missing words. Remember to add the letter **s** to show there is more than one thing.

a I have one cat.

I have two _____.

b Here is a sock.

Here is a pair of _____.

UNIT 6

The **short /e/** phoneme can be heard at the start of a word, such as 'egg'.

It can also be heard in the middle of a word, such as 'bet'.

1 Say the word you can see in the picture. Can you hear the **short /e/** vowel phoneme? Colour the pictures with the phoneme **/e/**. Write the letter **e** below those pictures.

_____ _____ _____ _____ _____

2 Say each word. Can you hear the phoneme **/e/**? Circle the words that have the phoneme **/e/**.

pet   ten   dad   got   get   did   pen

sat   pick   net   pot   pack   peck

dog   sock   neck   dot   kick   bat

pin   bet   sack   spit

3 Say each word again. What is the short vowel phoneme? Write one correct word in each box.

A word with a **short /a/**	A word with a **short /o/**

A word with a **short /i/**	A word with a **short /e/**

4 Make words that end with **et**. Say the onset letter, add the letters **et** and make a word. Write the word then say it.

Onset	Rime	Word
s		
n		
g	et	
p		
m		

OXFORD UNIVERSITY PRESS

1 Read each sentence. Say both words in the boxes. Circle the correct word.

a   I can | **kick** | | **kic** | .

b   I can | **gat** | | **get** | sick.

c   My | **pet** | | **pat** | dog is ten.

2 Find the words in the word search.

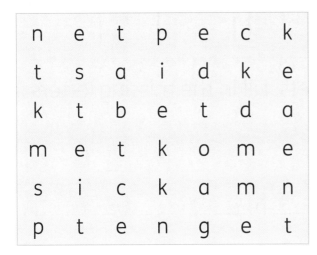

n	e	t	p	e	c	k
t	s	a	i	d	k	e
k	t	b	e	t	d	a
m	e	t	k	o	m	e
s	i	c	k	a	m	n
p	t	e	n	g	e	t

sick   said
net   me
met   ten
get   am
peck

3 Write each word twice.

OXFORD WORDLIST

look ► say ► cover ► write ► check

get			
me			
ten			

1 Write the missing words. Count the nets to help you. Remember to add the letter **s** to the end of the word to show there is more than one thing.

There is one net.

Now there are _____ _____

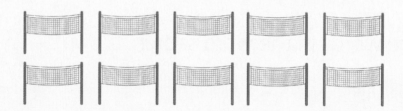

2 Look at the picture. Count the nets. Fill in the missing letters in this sentence:

I can count t_____ n_____ .

3 Look at the picture. Read the sentences. Write the missing letters.

I have a pet dog and a pet cat. I like my p_____.

OXFORD UNIVERSITY PRESS

Tip

The **short /u/** phoneme can be heard at the start of a word, such as 'up'.

It can also be heard in the middle of a word, such as 'sun'.

1 Say the word you can see in the picture. Can you hear the **short /u/** vowel phoneme? Colour the pictures with the **short /u/** phoneme. Write the letter **u** below those pictures.

_____   _____   _____   _____   _____

2 Say each word. Can you hear the phoneme **/u/**? Circle the words that have the phoneme **/u/**. Then draw a line under the words with the **short /a/** phoneme.

mum	tan	up	pack
cup	mad	pan	cut
nut	stack	duck	dad

3 Look at the pictures and answer the questions.

a Is it a bat or is it a bed?

It is a _____.

b Is it a cup or is it a cap?

It is a _____.

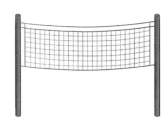

c Is it a nut or is it a net?

It is a _____.

d Is it a sack or is it a stick?

It is a _____.

e Is it a dog or is it a duck?

It is a _____.

1 Write each word twice.

OXFORD WORDLIST

look ⟶ say ⟶ cover ⟶ write ⟶ check

up		
mum		
my		
me		
said		
like		
go		
got		
to		
as		

1 Look at the pictures. Use them to help you write the missing words.

a   The two red _____

b   The ten big _____

c   Mum and Dad like to eat _____.

UNIT 8

1 Say the word you can see in the picture. Can you hear the phoneme **/r/**? Colour the pictures with the phoneme **/r/**. Write the letter **r** below those pictures.

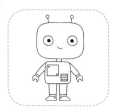     

_____ _____ _____ _____ _____ _____

2 Say each word. How many phonemes can you hear? Circle the words with three phonemes. Draw a line under the words with four phonemes.

rat	run	crack	ran	pram
rip	red	truck	rot	drag
rock	trick	trap	trip	

3 Look at the words above. Write the letter that stands for the **/r/** phoneme.

_____

OXFORD UNIVERSITY PRESS

My Family Helps Me
by Gordon Coutts

My grandma helps me get dressed.
My grandpa helps me get breakfast.

4 Write three words that have the **/r/** phoneme. Use the sentences above, or a book that you are reading in class.

_____   _____

_____

1 Find the words in the word search.

t	r	i	c	k	c	k	t	r	i
r	t	t	r	i	p	a	r	a	t
u	b	g	r	u	b	a	s	g	r
r	e	s	t	s	d	d	r	o	p
g	r	u	n	m	r	e	d	a	k
t	t	d	t	r	a	c	k	c	o
t	r	u	c	k	t	r	e	c	k
r	i	p	p	e	t	r	a	p	r

rat	trap
run	trip
rip	truck
red	trick
rest	track
drop	

2 Write each word twice.

look → say → cover → write → check

rats		
top		

3 Use 'rats' and 'top' to fill the gaps in this sentence.

Two _____ sat on

_____ of the red mat.

A base word is the smallest part of a word that is also a word on its own.

A suffix can be added to the end of a base word to make a new word.

For example: 'cat' is a base word and **-s** is a suffix. We add the suffix **-s** to show that there is more than one cat. This is called a plural.

Tip

1 Circle the plural word in each sentence. Write the base word.

Plural word	Base word
Here are two taps.	
Ten ants got sick.	
The rat has two red eyes.	
Dan has two pet dogs.	
Sam had ten pots.	
I do like nuts.	

UNIT 9

1 Say the word you can see in the picture. Can you hear the phoneme **/h/**? Colour the pictures with the phoneme **/h/**. Write the letter **h** below those pictures.

_____ _____ _____ _____ _____ _____

2 These words all start with the phoneme **/h/**. Write the letter **h** on each line. Then say each word.

_____im _____ot _____ it _____ad _____ug

_____and _____op _____en _____at _____em

A consonant is a sound you make with your lips, tongue or teeth. The phonemes **/b/**, **/g/**, **/d/**, **/p/**, **/k/** and **/t/** are examples of consonants.

You use your voice to say the consonants **/b/**, **/g/** and **/d/**. These are called voiced phonemes.

You use your breath to say the consonants **/p/**, **/k/** and **/t/**. These are called unvoiced phonemes.

Use your breath to say the first phoneme in these words:

p-at **t**-ag

Tip

My Family Helps Me
by Gordon Coutts

My dad helps me paint pictures.
My mum helps me ride my bike.

3 Listen carefully to these sentences as they are read out.
Find the word that has the consonant phonemes **/h/**, **/s/**, **/p/**.
Write the word below.

The word is: _____.

1 Find the words in the word search.

i	a	h	e	h	u	t	s
h	i	d	o	n	i	t	k
i	m	h	i	m	h	o	t
h	i	t	t	a	h	i	s
d	o	h	a	t	i	c	k
m	c	h	e	r	h	a	s
k	h	i	p	a	e	c	t
h	a	d	a	d	h	u	p

he	her	hot
him	had	hid
hit	has	hip
his	hat	hut

OXFORD UNIVERSITY PRESS

2 Read each sentence. Say both words in the boxes.
Circle the correct word.

He | **hit** | **hut** | the ball.   The pan is | **hat** | **hot** | .

3 Write each word twice.

look ➤ say ➤ cover ➤ write ➤ check

he		
him		
hit		
his		
her		
had		
has		

1 Read the base word. Write the plural word on each line.

Base word	Missing word
hat	I have two red _____ .
hand	I use both _____ to pat the cat.

Morphology

Tip

Look at the letters **b** and **d**. To help you remember the difference, look at the first and last letters in the word 'bed'.

1 Say the word you can see in the picture. Can you hear the phoneme **/b/**? Colour the pictures with the phoneme **/b/**. Write the letter **b** below those pictures.

_____ _____ _____ _____ _____ _____

2 Write the letter **b** on each line below. Read the words.

Mr McGee and the Big Bag of Bread

by Pamela Allen

Mr McGee stretched out in his _____ed.

He gave a _____ig yawn ...

Shall I stay in _____ed, or go out to play?

Mr McGee had a _____ig _____ag of _____read.

Do not feed the animals, the notice _____oard said.

3 Listen to your teacher read from a book. Write down two words that have the consonant phoneme **/b/**. Write down two words that have the consonant phoneme **/d/**.

/b/ as in 'bag'	/d/ as in 'dog'

1 Find the words in the word search.

d	a	s	b	u	s	g	e
c	k	p	i	o	b	a	t
e	b	e	s	t	e	t	b
b	i	g	i	g	b	u	t
d	e	b	r	e	a	d	b
o	b	a	c	k	e	c	k
a	g	b	b	a	g	i	g
r	b	e	d	b	i	d	h

but   bat
big   bag
back   bus
best   bread
bed

2 Write each word twice in the table on the next page.

OXFORD ★ WORDLIST   look ⟶ say ⟶ cover ⟶ write ⟶ check

but		
big		
back		
best		
bed		
bat		
bag		
bus		

1 Listen as your teacher reads the sentence below. Circle the homophones.

The bee will be making honey.

2 Read each sentence. Look at the homophones in the boxes. Colour the one that makes sense. Write the sentence using the correct homophone.

a The rat will [**be**] [**bee**] sick.

_____

b The [**be**] [**bee**] rests on the pot.

---

3 Read the base word. Write the plural word in each sentence. Draw a picture to match.

Base word	Plural word	Picture
bat	The two big _____ are black.	
bag	Dad has lots of _____.	
bed	The big hut has two _____.	

Phonology

Consonant digraphs are two letters that stand for one consonant sound.

Here are some consonant digraphs:

sh	As in '**sh**ips'	
ch	As in '**ch**ips'	

Tip

1 Say the word you can see in the picture. Can you hear the phoneme **/sh/**? Colour the pictures with the **/sh/** phoneme. Write the letters **sh** below those pictures.

_____ _____ _____ _____ _____

2 Say the word you can see in the picture. Can you hear the phoneme **/ch/**? Colour the pictures with the phoneme **/ch/**. Write the letters **ch** below those pictures.

_____ _____ _____ _____ _____

OXFORD UNIVERSITY PRESS

A Squash and a Squeeze
by Julia Donaldson

A table and _____airs

and a jug on the _____elf

The goat _____ewed the curtains.

_____e pu_____ed out the cow.

3 Use these words to help you to write the missing digraphs (**sh** or **ch**) in the sentences above.

| shelf | chairs | She | pushed | chewed |

1 Write each word twice.

OXFORD WORDLIST   look ⟶ say ⟶ cover ⟶ write ⟶ check

she		
shop		
much		

Orthography

2 On each line, write your own list of words to learn.

  a Words with the **sh** digraph:

  _____ _____ _____

  b Words with the **ch** digraph:

  _____ _____ _____

3 Oops! Correct the mistake in each sentence. Circle the correct word. Write the correct word.

	Circle one		Write the correct word
Hse sat on the mat.	Hse	She	
I like to eat hot hcips.	hcips	chips	
He hsut the back door.	hsut	shut	
Dad likes to hcat with Mum.	hcat	chat	

OXFORD UNIVERSITY PRESS

The suffix **-s** can be added to the end of some base words to tell us that something is happening.

In the sentence 'The dog runs', the **-s** tells you that the dog is running.

1 Read each sentence. Use the base word to help you write the missing word in each sentence. Remember to add the suffix **-s**.

Base word	Missing 'happening word'
nap	The cat _____ on the rug.
chop	Her dad _____ the nuts.
chat	His mum _____ to Nan.
rest	Anika _____ on the bed.
stop	The bus _____ at the shop.
sit	He _____ on the chair.
run	She _____ to the park.

Tip

Remember that a consonant digraph is when two letters stand for one consonant sound.

sh	as in 'ships'	
ch	as in 'chips'	
th	as in 'thumb'	
th	as in 'feather'	

1 Say the word you can see in the picture. Did you use your breath to say the **/th/** sound? This is called the unvoiced **/th/** phoneme. Colour the pictures with the unvoiced **/th/** phoneme. Write the letters **th** below those pictures.

_____   _____   _____   _____   _____

2 The words below have a voiced **/th/** phoneme. You need to use your voice to say this sound. Write the letters **th** below. Then say each word.

___ ___at   ___ ___en   ___ ___em   ___ ___is

3 Say each word. Is the **/th/** sound voiced or unvoiced? Circle the words with the voiced **/th/** phoneme. Draw a line under the words with the unvoiced **/th/** phoneme.

the   broth   this   thick   that

moth   then   cloth   them   thin

1 Write each word twice.

look → say → cover → write → check

the		
this		
that		
they		
then		
them		
with		

2 Look for these words in a book you are reading. Write a sentence from the book that has each word.

the	
this	
that	
they	

1 Write the missing words. Add the suffix **-s** to the base word to show that something is happening.

Base word	Missing 'happening word'
tick	The big clock _____ .
like	The dog _____ to run.
run	The rat _____ to the tap.
drop	She _____ the bag.
hit	He _____ the ball into the sky.

OXFORD UNIVERSITY PRESS

1 Say the word you can see in the picture. Can you hear the phoneme **/f/**? Colour the pictures with the phoneme **/f/**. Write the letter **f** below those pictures.

  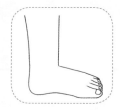  

_____   _____   _____   _____   _____

2 Say the word you can see in the picture. Can you hear the phoneme **/v/**? Colour the pictures with the phoneme **/v/**. Write the letter **v** below those pictures.

_____   _____   _____   _____

3 Say each word. Can you hear the voiced **/v/** phoneme or the unvoiced **/f/** phoneme? Write a word in each box on the next page.

vet   fat   flat   vest   fun   van

fist   have   flick   fret

A word with /f/ (unvoiced)	A word with /v/ (voiced)

If a word ends with a **/v/** phoneme, **it usually ends with the letters** ve.

1 Look for these words in a book you are reading.
Write a sentence from the book that has each word.

of	
have	
for	

2 Write each word twice.

look ⟶ say ⟶ cover ⟶ write ⟶ check

fun		
from		
if		

after		
off		
of		
have		
love		
very		

1 Each pair of words below are homophones. They sound the same but look different and have a different meaning.

Write the missing word by using the correct homophone.

for	four	The vet pats the _____ sick dogs.
eye	I	Stan likes dogs but _____ like frogs.
to	two	I like _____ run.

Phonology

1 Say the word you can see in the picture. Can you hear the phoneme **/l/** ? Colour the pictures with the phoneme **/l/**. Write the letter **l** below those pictures.

_____   _____   _____   _____   _____

2 Use these onsets and rimes to make words.

Onset	Rime	Word
f		
gr		
dr	ill	
ch		
thr		

Onset	Rime	Word
s		
t	ell	
sh		
sm		

Onset	Rime	Word
c		
b		
f	all	
t		
sm		

1 Use these words to write the missing words.

lots   All   call

Tip

Remember that a sentence always starts with an upper-case letter.

a _____ of the frogs have big red eyes.

b The shop has _____ of red and black hats to sell.

c I will have to _____ my mum and dad.

2 Write each word twice.

look → say → cover → write → check

lots		
all		
will		

1 The words 'no' and 'know' are homophones. They sound the same but look different and have a different meaning.

no   know

One of these homophones uses two letters to stand for the phoneme **/n/**. This is a consonant digraph. Circle the digraph.

2 Write the homophone 'no' in these sentences.

a The pot has _____ lid on top.

b I had a red bag but now I have _____ red bags.

3 Write the homophone 'know' in these sentences.

a Did the vet _____ that the cat is black?

b The vet did not _____ that the cat is black.

UNIT 15

1 Read these words out loud.

mess	will	less	fell	all	fuss

tall	miss	bell	dress	call	press

In these words, the letters **ss** stand for the phoneme **/s/**. The letters **ll** stand for the phoneme **/l/**. Circle the words that end with **/s/**. Draw a line under the words that end with **/l/**.

2 Use these onsets and rimes to make words.

Onset	Rime	Word
l		
m		
ch	ess	
dr		
pr		

Onset	Rime	Word
m		
k		
h	iss	
bl		

1 Say these words. Then use them in the sentences.

| so | some |

a I will have _____ bags of sticks.

b I am tired _____ I will go to bed.

2 Find the words in the word search.

t	h	i	m	w	i	t	h
h	s	m	i	s	s	i	g
a	s	u	s	o	m	h	r
e	c	a	l	c	a	l	l
t	h	o	s	o	m	e	y
e	y	t	h	e	y	o	p
m	e	s	s	o	m	c	e
s	l	o	p	l	o	t	s

so	miss
lots	mess
some	they
call	with

3 Write each word twice.

look ···▸ say ···▸ cover ···▸ write ···▸ check

so		
some		
they		

OXFORD UNIVERSITY PRESS

A compound word is a new word made out of two words joined together.

The word 'pancake' is a compound word made out of the words 'pan' and 'cake'.

Tip

1 Join these words to make compound words.

Base words		Compound word
up	on	
in	to	
week	end	

2 Use these compound words to write the missing words.

upon   into   weekend

a I went to the shops on the _____.

b The ball fell _____ the well.

c Once _____ a time, there was a big bad rat.

Now try the 'Bringing it together' activity, which your teacher will give you.

1 Draw a line to match each picture and word. Colour the pictures with the phoneme **/w/**.

 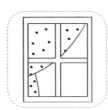  

| window | web | wheel | violin |

2 Use these onsets and the rimes to make words.

Onset	Rime	Word
b		
s		
r	ent	
v		
w		

Tip

The phoneme **/w/** can be written as:

w	as in 'wet'
wh	as in 'what'

1 Say each word. What letter or letters stand for the phoneme **/w/**? Circle the words with the letter **w**. Draw a line under the words with the letters **wh**.

wet   whisk   win   web   where

what   was   we   when

2 Can you find words with the phoneme **/w/** in a book you are reading? Write three of these words.

_____   _____   _____

3 Write each word twice.

OXFORD ★ WORDLIST   look ---> say ---> cover ---> write ---> check

we		
with		
went		
want		
will		
when		

what	
was	
were	

Morphology

1 The words 'where' and 'wear' are homophones. They sound the same but look different and have a different meaning.

| where | wear |

a Write the homophone 'where' in this sentence.

Mum, _____ will the bus stop?

b Write the homophone 'wear' in this sentence.

I like to _____ red socks.

Now try
the 'Bringing it
together' activity,
which your teacher
will give you.

UNIT 17

1 Draw a line to match each picture and word. Colour the pictures with the phoneme **/j/**.

| bridge | cat | jug | jelly |

2 Use these onsets and rimes to make words.

Onset	Rime	Word
b		
f		
n	udge	
j		
gr		

Onset	Rime	Word
r		
br	idge	
fr		

Tip

The **/j/** phoneme can be written in different ways. Here are two ways:

j	as in 'jug'
dge	as in 'bridge'

1 Say each word. Which letter or letters stand for the **/j/** phoneme? Circle the words with the letter **j**. Draw a line under the words with the letters **dge**.

jam   fudge   jet   nudge   jump

badge   bridge   just   fridge

Tip

A trigraph is three letters standing for one phoneme. The letters **dge** are a trigraph in the word 'dodge'.

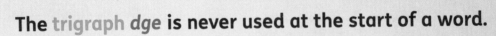

The trigraph dge is never used at the start of a word.

2 Can you find words with the **/j/** phoneme in a book you are reading? Write three of these words below.

_____ _____ _____

3 Find the words in the word search.

e	r	f	r	i	e	n	d
g	b	r	i	d	g	e	g
o	n	c	e	u	n	t	s
m	i	d	g	e	j	a	m
r	e	a	r	a	r	e	j
j	u	g	i	g	u	d	g
r	f	r	i	d	g	e	f

jug   once

fridge   friend

jam   are

bridge

4 Write each word twice.

look → say → cover → write → check

once		
friend		
are		

Happy Diwali
by Janine Scott

We make lamps for the festival. They are made of clay.

5 Copy the sentence above that has the word 'are'.

_____

_____

1 The words 'to', 'two' and 'too' are homophones. They sound the same but look different and have a different meaning.

to	two	too

a Read this sentence. Write the homophone 'to' on the line.

Jack and Jill went up the hill _____ fetch a pail of water.

b Read this sentence. Write the homophone 'two' on the line.

Jamila and Jen are _____ of my friends.

c Read this sentence. Write the homophone 'too' on the line.

Jim said that there is _____ much fudge in the fridge.

2 Look for these homophones in a book you are reading. Write a sentence from your book that has each word.

to	
too	

Now try the 'Bringing it together' activity, which your teacher will give you.

UNIT 18

1 Say the word you can see in the picture. Listen to the last phoneme in each word. It is written as a digraph: **ng**. Draw a line to match each picture and word. Colour the pictures.

| swing | ring | wing | king |

2 Use these onsets and rimes to make words.

Onset	Rime	Word
th	ing	
b	ang	
str	ong	
s	ung	

3 Add an onset to each rime below and on the next page. Write a sentence using that word. The first one has been done for you.

Rime	Sentence
string	I have a ball of string.
_____ang	

_____ong	
_____ung	

The *ng* digraph **is never used at the start of a word.**

1 Find the words in the word search.

b	d	o	b	r	i	n	g	m	g
s	a	w	n	g	o	i	n	g	p
g	h	a	v	e	n	p	u	t	n
r	e	b	a	n	g	w	a	s	e
e	l	n	g	l	i	t	t	l	e
a	y	h	t	t	h	e	y	i	m
t	a	t	g	p	u	t	s	c	k
s	d	s	a	i	d	f	r	n	g

bang	little
bring	put
going	said
do	they
saw	have

2 Write each word twice.

OXFORD WORDLIST

look ····► say ····► cover ····► write ····► check

going		
do		
saw		

little		
put		

3 Look for these words in a book you are reading. Write a sentence from your book that has each word.

do	
little	

1 Read the sentence out loud. Circle the homophones. They sound the same but look different and have a different meaning.

I won one tub of fudge.

Use these homophones to write the missing words.

no   know   one   won

a Don will pick _____ red hat.

b Min _____ a bat and ball.

c The ducks do not _____ where the pond is.

d There is _____ fudge left in the fridge.

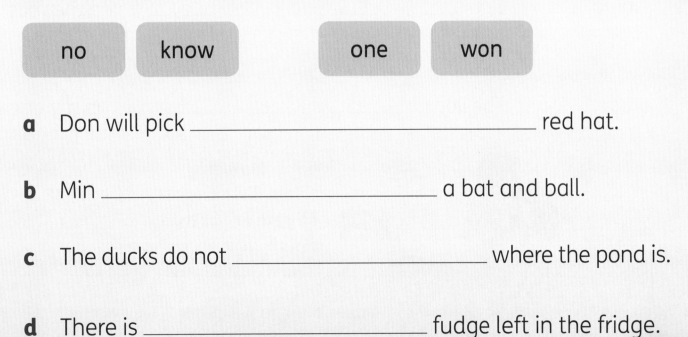

2 Which of these words end with the suffix **-ing**? Circle the words that end with **-ing**.

| jump | helping | run | skip | going | standing |

3 Add the suffix **-ing** to each base word. Write the missing happening word in the space.

Base word	Missing happening word
go	We are _____ on a bear hunt.
jump	I am _____ on the mat.
roar	The lion is _____ in my ear.

Now try the 'Bringing it together' activity, which your teacher will give you.

OXFORD UNIVERSITY PRESS

1 Say the word you can see in the picture. Can you hear the phoneme **/z/** ? Colour the pictures with the phoneme **/z/**. Write the letter **z** below those pictures.

_____ _____ _____ _____

> Tip
>
> In some words, the letter **s** stands for the phoneme **/z/**.

2 Say each word. Can you hear the phoneme **/z/** or **/s/**? Circle the words with **/z/**. Draw a line under the words with **/s/**. Then write one word in each box.

| soft | zebra | sick | his | zap |

| split | hiss | bins | mess | was | stop |

A word with **/z/** (voiced)	A word with **/s/** (unvoiced)

3 Use these onsets and rimes to make words.

Onset	Rime	Word
sn	atch	
scr		

Onset	Rime	Word
sw	itch	
tw		

Onset	Rime	Word
f	etch	
sk		

4 Add an onset to each rime. Write a sentence using that word.

_____atch	
_____itch	
_____etch	

The **zz digraph is never used at the start of a word.**

OXFORD UNIVERSITY PRESS

1 Say each word. Which letter or letters are used to stand for the phoneme **/z/**? Circle the words with the letter **z**. Draw a line under the words with the letters **zz**.

buzz	fizz	zip	zebra	whiz

> **Tip**
>
> The **tch** trigraph stands for the sound **/ch/**. These letters are never used at the start of a word.

2 Say each word. What letters are used to stand for the phoneme **/ch/**? Write the word in the correct box.

catch	chess	chat	stitch

Words with **ch**	Words with **tch**

3 Write each word twice.

OXFORD WORDLIST   look → say → cover → write → check

family		
favourite		
sister		

4 Look for this word in a book you are reading.
Write a sentence from your book that has the word.

family

1 Read the base words and sentences below. They are based on two books called *My Family Helps Me*, by Gordon Coutts, and *The Dentist Can Help You*, by George Ivanoff. Check if you need to add **-ing** or **-s** to the base word to make the missing word in the sentence.

Base word	Sentence
help	My family will _____ me.
	My family _____ me.
	My sister is _____ me.

Base word	Sentence
clean	The dentist will _____ your teeth.
	The dentist _____ your teeth.
	The dentist is _____ your teeth.

Now try the 'Bringing it together' activity, which your teacher will give you.

66

UNIT 20

> When speech sounds are joined together it is called a blend.
>
> When you see the letters **qu** in a word, they stand for a blend of the phonemes **/k/** and **/w/**.
>
> The letters **qu** stand for the blend **/kw/**.

1 Say each word. Circle the letters **qu**. Count the number of phonemes in each word.

Words with **qu**	How many phonemes?
quick	
liquid	
quiz	

2 Read these words out loud. What blend can you hear at the start? Sort the words into the boxes.

| clap | quack | click | queen | quick | clash |

The blend is _____	The blend is _____

1 Find the words in the word search.

g	f	r	q	u	a	c	k	e	k
q	u	b	e	c	a	u	s	e	v
a	r	e	s	q	u	a	r	e	q
q	u	a	f	a	m	i	l	y	v
q	e	e	n	q	u	e	e	n	b
d	f	a	v	o	u	r	i	t	e
c	k	u	q	u	q	u	i	c	k
z	s	q	u	a	s	h	a	b	k

queen   favourite

quick   family

quack   because

2 Write each word twice.

look ➤ say ➤ cover ➤ write ➤ check

because	
queen	

3 Circle the first letter of every word in this sentence:

Big elephants can always understand small elephants.

These letters spell the word 'because'.
The sentence gives you a trick for
remembering how to spell 'because'.

4 Write a sentence using the words 'queen' and 'because'.

_____

_____

1 Read the base word. Use it to write the missing word in each sentence. Check if you need to add **-ing** or **-s** to make the missing word.

Base word	Sentence
quack	The duck can _____ .
	The duck _____ .
	The duck is _____ .

Tip

Happening words are called verbs. 'Play' is the verb in the sentence 'I play chess'.

2 Some words end in the letters **ing** but they are not happening words. How can you tell? Say the words below. Are they naming words or happening words? Circle the happening words.

wing   bending   ring   stretching   jumping   king

Now try the 'Bringing it together' activity, which your teacher will give you.

1 Say the word you can see in the picture. If you can you hear the consonant phoneme **/y/** write the letter **y** below.

_____ _____ _____

2 Write the letter **y** to complete the words in these sentences.

a I _____awn when I am sleepy.

b The box is _____ellow.

3 Use these onsets and rimes to make words.

Onset	Rime	Word
f		
m	ix	
s		

Onset	Rime	Word
f		
b	ox	

4 Use these words to fill in the spaces below.

Max   fox   mix   box   six

a _____ is my friend and he is _____ years old.

b I can _____ red and yellow paint.

c The red _____ is running.

d The hat is in the _____.

1 Write each word twice.

look ⟶ say ⟶ cover ⟶ write ⟶ check

yes		
you		
your		
next		

2 Look for these words in a book you are reading.
Write a sentence from your book that has each word.

you	
your	

> **Tip**
>
> The suffix **-ed** can be added to a base word to tell us that something has happened in the past. Sometimes you can hear the **/t/** phoneme at the end of these words.

Alexander's Outing
by Pamela Allen

Alexander's mother quacked and quacked. And all his brothers and sisters quacked and quacked and flapped and flapped.

1 Read the sentences above. Circle the verbs (happening words) that end in the suffix **-ed**.

2 Read the base word. Do you need to add the suffix **-ing** or **-ed** to make the missing word in the sentence?

Base word	Sentence
quack	Yesterday, the duck _____.
	The duck is _____.

OXFORD UNIVERSITY PRESS

3 Read each word. Does it end with the suffix **-ed**? Or is it a base word? Write it in the correct box. The first one has been done for you.

quack   jump   ended   plant   landed

Base word	Base word with **-ed** suffix
quack	quack**ed**
	jumped
land	
end	
	planted

Now try this unit's 'Bringing it together' activity, which your teacher will give you.

A diphthong is a kind of long vowel sound.

Slowly say the word 'cow'. The shape of your mouth changes as you say the end of the word.

Tip

The sound **/ow/** in 'mouse' is a diphthong.

1 Read these words out loud. What vowel sound do they have? Write them in the correct box.

cow

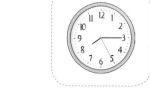

clock

red

hat

/ow/ sound	**Short /a/** vowel

Short /e/ vowel	**Short /o/** vowel

OXFORD UNIVERSITY PRESS

2 Read this sentence. Circle the two **ow** letter patterns. They are both spelled **ow** but they sound different.

This cow will be at the show.

3 Use these onsets and rimes to make words.

Onset	Rime	Word
c		
h	ow	
n		

Onset	Rime	Word
l		
gl	ow	
bl		

1 Say these words. They all have the same vowel sound. The digraphs **ow** and **ou** stand for the same sound in these words. Circle the words with the letters **ow**. Draw a line under the words with the letters **ou**.

sound   town   out   round   brown   now

how   about   crown   howl   proud   gown

OXFORD UNIVERSITY PRESS

The digraph **ow** can be used to stand for different diphthongs.

For example, we write 'how' and 'throw' using **ow**, but we say them differently.

2 Find the words in the word search.

n	u	f	o	u	n	d	o	w	e
e	t	f	o	u	a	b	o	u	t
t	h	r	t	o	w	n	b	h	e
x	h	o	u	s	e	h	u	o	s
o	u	w	g	p	n	o	w	f	r
f	l	h	o	w	o	u	t	g	k
n	o	u	d	o	w	n	o	u	r

now   out

how   about

down   found

town

3 Write each word twice.

look ⟶ **say** ⟶ **cover** ⟶ **write** ⟶ **check**

now		
how		
down		
town		
out		
about		
found		

1 Use the base word to help you to write the missing word in the sentences. Do you need to add the suffix **-ing** or **-ed**?

Base word	Sentence
rush	The mouse is _____ . The mouse _____ into the house.
howl	As the dog stood on the log, it _____ . The dog is _____ as it stands on the log.
follow	The dog _____ us this morning. The dog is _____ us down the path.
wish	He is _____ to pat the cat. He _____ to pat the cat.
yell	When the ride went fast, the kids _____ . The kids are _____ on the fast ride.

Now try this unit's 'Bringing it together' activity, which your teacher will give you.

UNIT 23

Another diphthong is the sound **/oi/**. Slowly say the word 'toy'. Can you feel your mouth change shape as you say the end of the word?

1 Say each word. What diphthong can you hear? Write the word in the correct box.

| coin | yellow | snow | toy | toilet | arrow |

/oi/ as in 'boy'	
long /o/ as in 'glow'	

2 Use these onsets and rimes to make words.

Onset	Rime	Word
j		
t	oy	
b		

OXFORD UNIVERSITY PRESS

Onset	Rime	Word
sw		
pl	ay	
spr		

1 Say each word. The digraphs **oy** and **oi** are used to stand for the same sound. Write one word in each box.

toy   point

A word with **oy**	A word with **oi**

2 Write each word twice.

OXFORD WORDLIST   look ▸ say ▸ cover ▸ write ▸ check

hand		
jump		
kind		
toy		
day		

1 Use the base word to help you write the missing word in these sentences. Do you need to add the suffix **-ing** or **-ed**?

Base word	Sentence
point	Leroy is _____ at the toys.
	Yesterday, Leroy _____ at the toys.
annoy	The noisy birds are _____ me.
	Last week, the birds _____ me.
play	I _____ with my friends all day.
	I enjoy _____ with my friends.

Now try this unit's 'Bringing it together' activity, which your teacher will give you.

OXFORD UNIVERSITY PRESS

UNIT 24

1 Say each word. What is the vowel phoneme in each word? Circle the words with the **short /a/** phoneme. Draw a line under the words with the **long /a/** phoneme.

| cake | cat | spray | fan |

| rain | hat | train | bat |

2 Use these onsets and rimes to make words.

Onset	Rime	Word
s		
m		
b	ay	
st		
str		

Onset	Rime	Word
br		
gr		
st	ain	
spr		

Tip

A split digraph is two vowel letters with a consonant letter in the middle. The two vowel letters stand for one vowel sound.

There is a split digraph (**a-e**) in the word 'cake'.

1 Say these words. Which letters stand for the vowel phoneme? Write the word in the correct box.

play   ate   train   stay   name   plain

Words with **ay**	Words with **ai**	Words with **a-e**

2 Find the words in the word search.

s	k	o	y	s	p	l	a	y	h
f	r	c	o	b	w	a	y	o	i
h	c	a	m	e	m	e	c	a	g
o	w	f	r	a	m	a	k	e	g
t	e	a	n	t	c	h	d	a	y
n	a	i	m	n	m	a	d	e	v
z	a	y	f	n	a	m	e	o	y

way   made
play   name
day   came
make

3 Write each word twice.

look ▸ say ▸ cover ▸ write ▸ check

way		
play		
day		
make		
made		
name		
came		

OXFORD UNIVERSITY PRESS

1 Read the sentence and circle the homophones.

Eight children ate the grapes.

2 Write two sentences using the homophones 'ate' and 'eight'.

ate	
eight	

> The letter *s* can be added to a base word to make a plural. This shows that there is more than one thing.
>
> But if a base word ends in *s*, *x*, *z*, *ch* or *sh*, you need to add *-es* to make a plural.

3 Add **-es** to the following base words to make them plural.

Base word	Sentence
fox	There are two _____ at the zoo.
dish	They had to wash all of the _____ .
bench	We sit on _____ at the playground.
bus	The _____ all left the school.

Now try this unit's 'Bringing it together' activity, which your teacher will give you.

OXFORD UNIVERSITY PRESS

UNIT 25

1 Read each word out loud. What vowel sound does it have? Write the word in the correct box.

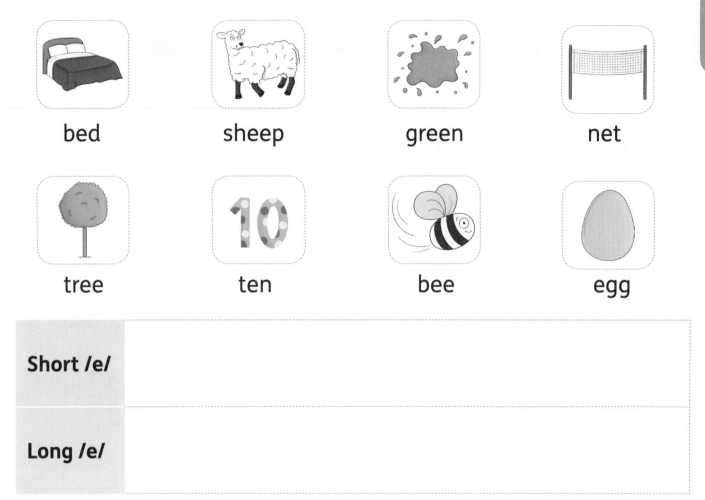

bed   sheep   green   net

tree   ten   bee   egg

Short /e/	
Long /e/	

2 Say each word. How many phonemes can you hear? Circle the words with three phonemes. Draw a line under the words with four phonemes.

sheep   greet   speak   need   treat   speed

mean   seat   fleet   teeth   sleep   three

3 Circle the letters that stand for the **long /e/** vowel phoneme in the above words.

1 Say each word. Which letters stand for the vowel sound? Write the word in the correct box.

eat   sleep   need   tea

teeth   speak   beach   three

Words with **ee**	Words with **ea**

2 Write each word twice.

look ▸ say ▸ cover ▸ write ▸ check

eat		
tea		
beach		
sleep		
need		
teeth		
three		

1 Read these sentences. Circle the homophones. They sound the same but look different and have a different meaning.

a We can see a ship out at sea.

b I will not eat the bean that has been left out all day.

2 Read the pairs of homophones. Choose the correct homophone to write as the missing word.

ate	eight	The cow _____ some fresh green grass.
been	bean	The sheep have _____ sleeping.
see	sea	I hope I will _____ you next week.

3 Write a sentence with each of these homophones.

see	
sea	
been	
bean	

4 Read these sentences. Write the missing base word on the line.

a There were many **toys** in the box.

Now there is one _____ in the box.

b We had many **seeds**.

Now there is one _____ left.

c The **foxes** were peering at the cat.

Now there is one _____ peering at the cat.

Now try this unit's 'Bringing
it together' activity, which your
teacher will give you.

OXFORD UNIVERSITY PRESS

UNIT 26

1 Say each word. What vowel sound does it have? Circle the words with the **short /o/** phoneme. Draw a line under the words with the **long /o/** phoneme.

clock   goat   nose   frog   hose   sock

2 Circle the last two letters in these words.

cow   blow   how   glow   show   now

What two letters do the words end with? _____ _____

3 Now say each word. What vowel phoneme can you hear? Write the word in the correct box. Read the examples to help you.

/ow/ as in 'cow'	**long /o/** as in 'glow'

4 Say each word. How many phonemes can you hear? Circle the words with three phonemes. Draw a line under the words with four phonemes.

| home | spoke | goat | nose | stove | hose |

| rope | broke | bone | globe | those | froze |

1 Say each word. Which letters stand for the vowel sound? Write the word in the correct box.

| row | no | float | home | go | those | flow | boat |

Words with **o**	Words with **oa**

Words with **ow**	Words with **o-e**

OXFORD UNIVERSITY PRESS

2 Find the words in the word search.

f	e	e	m	b	l	o	w
c	h	f	l	o	w	g	r
o	w	s	t	h	o	s	e
x	o	e	h	o	m	e	v
f	l	o	a	t	f	o	e
g	e	s	p	o	k	e	h
j	o	p	e	g	o	o	w
b	o	w	t	b	o	a	t

home   flow
float   go
those   blow
spoke   boat

3 Write each word twice.

look ⟶ say ⟶ cover ⟶ write ⟶ check

home		
ago		
eat		
sleep		
make		
day		

1 Look at the pictures to help you write the missing words.

a This is a _____ .

b These are _____ .

c This is a _____ .

d These are _____ .

e This is a _____ .

f These are _____ .

g This is a _____ .

h These are _____ .

Now try this unit's 'Bringing it together' activity, which your teacher will give you.

1 Say each word. What vowel sound can you hear? Circle the words with the **short /o/** phoneme. Draw a line under the words with the **long /oo/** phoneme.

| spoon | frog | broom | clock | moon | sock |

A vowel digraph is two letters standing for one vowel sound. The word 'week' has the vowel digraph **ee**.

2 Circle the vowel digraph in each word.

| look | room | good | broom |

| took | moon | soon | shook |

3 Say each word from the last activity. What vowel sound can you hear? Write the word in the correct box. Use the examples to help you.

Short /oo/ as in 'look'	**Long /oo/** as in 'room'

4 Say each word. How many phonemes can you hear? Circle the words with three phonemes. Draw a line under the words with four phonemes.

| broom | school | look | good | stood | food |

1 Say each word. Which letters stand for the vowel sound? Circle the words with **oo**. Draw a line under the words with **ew**.

| room | flew | moon | blew | grew | soon |

| tooth | chew | broom | screw | brew | spoon |

2 Write each word twice.

OXFORD WORDLIST

look ⟶ say ⟶ cover ⟶ write ⟶ check

look		
good		
school		

Wombat Stew

by Marcia Vaughan

toothy	stew	

'I'm	brewing	up	a	gooey,	chewy

		with	that	fat	wombat,'

replied	Dingo	with	a		grin.

3 Listen to your teacher read the sentences above. Point to each word as you hear it. Use the words above to fill the gaps.

Never Mail an Elephant

by Mike Thaler

The mailman went to the mailbox and opened the door.
Then he pulled…and tugged…and yanked the elephant out!

1 Listen to your teacher read these sentences. There are some verbs (happening words) that end in **-ed**. Circle the suffix **-ed** for these verbs.

> Now try the 'Bringing it together' activity, which your teacher will give you.

UNIT 28

1 Say each word. What vowel sound can you hear? Write the word in the correct box.

kite   ring   king   ice   nine

Short /i/	
Long /i/	

> **Tip**
>
> Rhyming words have the same ending sounds.
> For example, 'hat' and 'cat' are rhyming words.

2 Say each word. How many phonemes can you hear? Circle the words with three phonemes. Draw a line under the words with four phonemes.

like   bright   time   slide   ride   fright

side   glide   hide   light   flight

OXFORD UNIVERSITY PRESS

3 Say these words. Which long vowel sound do they have? Find the rhyming words. Write two rhyming words in each box.

| sky | dry | tea | boat | sea | away | afloat | day |

1 Say each word. What letter or letters stand for the **long /i/** vowel phoneme? Write the word in the correct box.

| fight | by | try | side | my |

| might | night | bite | ride |

y	
i-e	
igh	

Mr McGee Goes to Sea
by Pamela Allen

cry	sky	wide	fly	by	inside

The monster yawned and opened _____.

Poor Mr McGee went down _____.

The great fish gave a little _____.

'Oo! Ooo! Oooooo! I've swallowed a _____,'.

Mr McGee flew through the _____,

like a rocket racing _____.

2 Use the words to help you to fill in the missing words in the sentences above.

3 Write each word twice.

OXFORD ★ WORDLIST   look ⟶ say ⟶ cover ⟶ write ⟶ check

like		
time		
side		
ride		

OXFORD UNIVERSITY PRESS

hide		
light		

1 Write the missing plural words. Remember to add the suffix **-s** or **-es** to the base word to show there is more than one thing.

a There was only one **toy** in the box.

Now there are many _____ in the box.

b I had one **spoon**.

Now I have two _____.

c One **fox** was sleeping.

Now two _____ are sleeping.

d We had one **paint brush**.

Now we have nine paint _____.

e One **frog** jumped.

Then two _____ jumped into the pond.

f An **ant** went marching down the hill.

Then ten _____ went marching down the hill.

g There was one **boat** out at sea yesterday.

There are many _____ out at sea today.

GLOSSARY

base word	the smallest part of a word that is also a word on its own *the word 'jump' in 'jumping'*
blend	speech sounds that join together in a word **/st/** *is a blend in the word 'stop'*
compound word	a new word made out of two words joined together *sunshine (sun + shine), playground (play + ground)*
consonant	a speech sound made by blocking some air with your lips, teeth or tongue **/b/**, **/l/**, **/z/**, **/v/**
consonant digraph	two letters standing for one consonant sound **sh**, **ch**, **th**
digraph	two letters standing for one phoneme **sh**, **ch**, **oo**, **ee**, **ie**
diphthong	a kind of long vowel sound that you make by moving your mouth in two ways **/oi/** *in 'boy',* **/ow/** *in 'cow'*
homophone	a word that sounds the same as another word but looks different and has a different meaning *eight, ate*
medial phoneme	the speech sound in the middle of a word. This can be a medial vowel or a medial consonant. **/o/** *is the medial phoneme in the word 'dog'*
onset	the sounds in a word before the vowel **b** *stands for the onset in the word 'big'*

OXFORD UNIVERSITY PRESS

phoneme	the smallest speech sound you can hear in a word
	the word 'boot' has three phonemes: **/b/**, **long /oo/** *and* **/t/**
plural	a word for more than one thing
	'hats' is the plural of the word 'hat'
rime	the vowel and other speech sounds after the onset
	ig *stands for the rime in the word 'big'*
split digraph	two vowel letters standing for a speech sound, separated by a consonant letter
	a *and* **e** *in 'take' stand for a* **long /a/** *sound together*
suffix	letters that go at the end of a word to make a new word
	the **-s** *in 'cats' means 'more than one cat'*
trigraph	three letters standing for one phoneme **igh** *in 'might'*
unvoiced phoneme	a sound made using your breath rather than your voice
	/th/ *in 'bath'*
verb	a word for something that happens
	'play' is the verb in the sentence 'I play chess.'
voiced phoneme	a sound made using your voice
	/th/ *in 'the'*
vowel	a sound that you voice with your mouth open and not blocked by your lips, teeth or tongue
	the **short /o/** *sound in the word 'dog' is a vowel sound*
vowel digraph	two letters standing for one vowel sound
	ee, ay

OXFORD UNIVERSITY PRESS

When you have finished the activities in each unit, think about how you feel about the work you have completed.

Draw a ✓ if you feel confident using these ideas on your own.

Draw a ✗ if you feel you need to learn more.

Draw a O if you are not sure.

Unit	Phonology	Orthography	Morphology
1			
2			
3			
4			
5			
6			
7			
8			
9			
10			
11			
12			
13			
14			
15			
16			
17			
18			
19			
20			
21			
22			
23			
24			
25			
26			
27			
28			

OXFORD UNIVERSITY PRESS